Sex Yoga

The 7 Easy Steps To A Mind-Blowing Kundalini Awakening!

Sex Yoga

The 7 Easy Steps To A Mind-Blowing Kundalini Awakening!

S. F. Howe

Diamond Star Press

Los Angeles

Sex Yoga: The 7 Easy Steps To A Mind-Blowing Kundalini Awakening!

Copyright © 2018 S. F. Howe
Published by Diamond Star Press
Paperback Edition
ISBN 13: 978-1-7324591-0-6
ISBN 10: 1-73245-910-X

Books by S. F. Howe

Matrix Man
How To Become Enlightened, Happy And Free In An
Illusion World

The Top Ten Myths Of Enlightenment
Exposing The Truth About Spiritual Enlightenment
That Will Set You Free!

The Bringer
How To Free Yourself From The Mind Control
Programs Of The Matrix Reality
Coming Soon!

Secrets Of The Plant Whisperer
How To Care For, Connect, And Communicate With
Your House Plants

Your Plant Speaks!
How To Use Your Houseplant As A Therapist
Coming Soon!

Vision Board Success
How To Get Everything You Want With Vision
Boards!

Sex Yoga
The 7 Easy Steps To A Mind-Blowing Kundalini
Awakening!

Morning Routine For Night Owls
How To Supercharge Your Day With A Gentle Yet
Powerful Morning Routine!

Transgender America
Spirit, Identity, And The Emergence Of The Third
Gender

When Nothing Else Works
How To Cure Your Lower Back Pain Fast!

Acknowledgements

I wish to acknowledge my friend and fellow spiritual explorer, Jill Goss, who, a number of years ago, disclosed to me her interest in tantric massage of the chakras to invoke transcendent spiritual experiences. That conversation with Jill was the first time I had heard of this powerful technique and its profound implications, causing me to seek out more information. I discovered that this simple practice has long been alluded to in the tantric literature, but has not been given the status it deserves as a fast track to cosmic consciousness. Inspired by what I learned, I felt called to present this information to my readers so that you may benefit from its sexual healing potential as well as its ability to induce an ecstatic spiritual awakening.

Bonus Gift

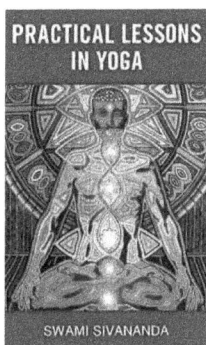

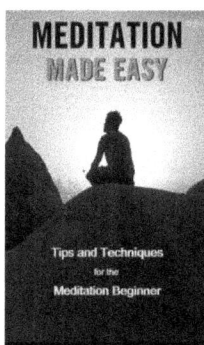

As my thanks to you for reading *Sex Yoga: The 7 Easy Steps To A Mind-Blowing Kundalini Awakening!*, I would like you to have a free starter library of two bonus ebooks, "Practical Lessons in Yoga" and "Meditation Made Easy." The information and techniques offered in these books perfectly complement *Sex Yoga*. Together, they will teach you how to quiet your mind, focus in the moment, strengthen your core and consciously move energy through your chakras. This will help assure your success with the technique presented in *Sex Yoga* and prepare you for the powerful energetic changes that occur when you attempt to raise your kundalini.

To receive your free gift, just send an email to info@diamondstarpress.com with proof of purchase and "Send Sex Yoga Gift" in the subject field, and we will get your starter library out to you right away. Do it now before you forget!

To the ones who seek to go higher,
for whom even Mount Everest is not high enough.

Table of Contents

Introduction to Sex Yoga

Wherefore you will receive in this book is the never before revealed, yet simple and complete Sex Yoga technique for experiencing the ultimate orgasm. I call it the kundalini orgasm – a prolonged, ecstatic sexual build-up that culminates in an orgasmic explosion of Light/energy out through the top of your head and into the farthest reaches of the cosmos as you blissfully merge with the All That Is.

This priceless experience is accomplished naturally and easily when you learn how to flow your own sexual energy through the seven chakras or power centers of your body. You may practice this technique alone or with a partner, although I recommend that you begin alone, if only to familiarize yourself with the steps and the incredible rapture of this mind-blowing sexual/spiritual adventure.

This is life-changing knowledge that I am sharing with you. I not only reveal everything you need to know to begin exploring and mastering the Sex Yoga technique, but you will also learn:

* How to prolong and extend your orgasms, not for a few more minutes but for hours!

* How to harness your own sexual energy to awaken your highest spirituality

* What your chakras are and why they are your fast track to enlightenment

* How the spiritual transformation you have been yearning for is literally at your fingertips

* How the kundalini orgasm not only brings incredible ecstasy to you and your partner but also eliminates pressure and stress from lovemaking

* Why the kundalini orgasm results in incomparable love and bonding with your partner

* How you can experience the heights of sexual ecstasy and spiritual bliss at any time, even without a partner in your life!

…and much, much more.

Do be patient with yourself and/or your partner as you practice the steps and increase your awareness and sensitivity to this process. Your efforts will be richly rewarded!

Chapter 1

Welcome to the Kundalini Orgasm

If you are like most of my readers, you have been in search of spiritual truth and enlightenment for many years. You may have studied Eastern philosophy, followed various gurus and tried numerous so-called New Age practices, such as meditation, yoga, visualization, affirmation, brainwave entrainment, law of attraction, etc. And possibly you have even attempted to raise your spiritual vibrations and extend your sexual pleasure with tantric practices.

But I also suspect that none of those paths brought you any significant or lasting results, much less the bliss and enlightenment you are seeking. So let's take a moment to imagine that you do have a permanent, life-altering spiritual awakening. But it doesn't happen while sitting cross-legged, meditating in the Zen-do, or performing the Sun Salutation on a beach; it occurs unexpectedly and spontaneously during an extraordinary sexual experience!

As the most delectable fruit of that awakening, you find yourself privy to information from a higher dimension. Among the secrets revealed to you is a certain method of using sexual energy as a portal to higher consciousness and Oneness with Source. This portal can be accessed either alone or with a partner. Entering the portal brings the most beatific and rapturous experience that you can have while still living in the physical world. Words cannot adequately describe this exalted experience, but for all practical purposes you refer to it as the kundalini orgasm.

You can rest assured that within these pages you will find everything you really need to know about the kundalini orgasm. I advise you to slowly and carefully read through this book, then read it again. After that, I strongly suggest that you put aside any doubts and questions, and simply try the technique! Much will be answered in so doing.

Let us begin.

Chapter 2

What is Kundalini?

Perhaps you have heard it said that at the base of your spine lies a coiled serpent whose mystical fire, when unleashed, whips up your spinal column and out the top of your head, delivering you to unparalleled ecstasy and enlightenment. Otherwise known as the awakened kundalini, which has its roots in ancient Indian meditational practices, the raised serpent force purports to transform every aspect of your existence into a higher state and give you unimaginable powers.

The promise of kundalini reads like the stuff of fantasy fiction and, as such, remains in the fantasy realm until you are fortunate enough to have the experience yourself. While you are preparing for that experience, the best thing to do is learn as much as you can about it.

Traditional concepts of kundalini point to a latent energy source within the human body that has the potential to reconfigure the body, mind and spirit of a human being, turning them into a more god-like being, i.e., one who is enlightened and able to transcend the limitations of this world. This belief has made kundalini the holy grail of spiritual seekers, sparking endless hours of study, meditation and yoga. It has also inspired many to become followers of the various gurus who offer a pathway to achieving enlightenment. This usually involves years of absorbing the guru's teachings, performing the required practices, and basking in his *shakti* transmissions.

The hunt for kundalini-fueled enlightenment is not unlike undertaking a search for Shangri-La, the mythical locale in the Himalayas where inhabitants live a perfect life in eternal youth. Many have heard the stories, but few know how to find it, what it is really like, and what gifts it actually does bestow on a seeker. This obfuscation leaves the seeker vulnerable to giving years of their life to ascetic spiritual practices, unscrupulous gurus and dead-end paths in their eagerness to become enlightened and experience the bliss of a raised kundalini.*

On the one hand, kundalini is idolized by those on the Eastern philosophy path as a shortcut to spiritual enlightenment – the pearl of great price that is forever sought yet rarely found. On the other hand, it is demonized by Fundamentalist Christians and other religious groups as a means of becoming possessed by an evil spirit. Between these two polarities are those who warn about the dangers of prematurely raising kundalini and caution you to make sure you are ready.

The abundant lore about kundalini is quite a lot to assimilate, especially if you are reading a book like this, which aims to lead you through the seven sacred steps to a kundalini orgasm. Obviously, how you view these matters is important for the ease and enjoyment of your journey, which therefore makes them worthy of consideration. We must ask hard questions and seek the highest answers.

In the next chapter we will answer the following questions: Is kundalini even real? Is it all that it is promised to be? Could it be a devil in sheep's clothing? What are the dangers of raising kundalini?

---

*If you would like more information about the many pitfalls of the spiritual path, please visit Amazon and check out my book, *The Top Ten Myths Of Enlightenment: Exposing The Truth About Spiritual Enlightenment That Will Set You Free!* Many read travel guides as a matter of course before visiting a foreign country. But when it comes to taking a spiritual journey there is a virtual blackout on helpful information. For this reason, I wrote *The Top Ten Myths Of Enlightenment.* I want you to feel supported on your spiritual journey and able to make more informed decisions so that you stay safe in your travels.

Chapter 3

Awakening Kundalini

Quantum physics reveals that we live in an invisible energy field of coded information, otherwise known as The Field. Our physical perception transforms this code into the material objects that appear in our outer reality. But this energy field not only contains the coding which allows us to perceive the physical objects of our three-dimensional world, it also constitutes the air we breathe and the space between molecules. In other words, it permeates everything.

In metaphysics, we have many names for The Field. For example, we may call it Consciousness, the Absolute, the All, the Universe, God or Source. But all of those different names refer to one thing: the First Cause of manifest reality and of our very Life Force itself. This Cause is Infinite, Unlimited and Omnipotent, presiding as a never-ending fountain of Life.

From this perspective we can access a higher concept of kundalini, one which reveals it to be real, natural and infinitely powerful. This kundalini *is* the very substance of God, of the Life Force itself, everywhere present and all-encompassing. It is simply the energy field constituting our reality and our physical being. However, it is also the case that individuals access different frequencies and amounts of this energy depending on their level of consciousness. That is why kundalini appears invisible and even inactive in the lives of most people; the majority are culturally programmed for a level of consciousness that does not permit its realization. Awakening to kundalini is identical to awakening to the Life Force perpetually permeating your entire being. It was always there waiting to be recognized.

An awakened kundalini is nothing more than the recognition of and surrender to the all-pervading presence of kundalini energy. This awakening may occur gradually or in full. It may occur when following the intense, pleasurable surges of energy through the chakras during meditation. It can happen while performing yoga poses designed to unblock and move energy through the chakras. Or it may occur spontaneously during sexual activity when the partners have ideal chemistry and resonance, and one or both are simply ready. Lastly, you can also coax it into expression by practicing specific tantric techniques such as the method we teach in this book.

Because a person's access to these higher energies is limited by their level of consciousness, most people do not recognize the presence of kundalini or of higher energies. The achieving of a full kundalini awakening, and receipt of all of its gifts, begins with becoming conscious of the existence of this higher energy and then opening to the experience that accompanies its realization through meditation and practice. While undergoing this process, you may achieve readiness at the subconscious level before having a conscious awareness of your readiness. In cases like that, the awakening appears to be spontaneous and unexpected, and therefore the recipient feels unprepared and, perhaps, even shocked. However, if one looks closer it becomes apparent that the individual is vibrating at the necessary frequency, and, therefore, has manifested a state of consciousness that allows for this experience. On the surface it may appear sudden, but spiritual sight shows an individual resonating at the level of a kundalini awakening.

Once the awakening occurs, what can one expect? As we know, superhuman abilities have long been attributed to those with an awakened kundalini, and often these gifts are related to the Sixth and Seventh Chakras, such as the gift of prophecy, of second sight, heightened intuition, and access to higher wisdom. The awakened one may believe they have become enlightened, having realized the truth about reality and their own identity as the All. Some of these individuals establish themselves as gurus by acquiring a cadre of followers who believe in their guru's spiritual completion and hope his enlightenment will rub off on them.

Unfortunately, belief and hope are not the same as truth. In reality, an awakening falls within a spectrum of frequencies, depending on the individual and their unique vibrational bandwidth. What this means is that awakening to kundalini is, for the vast majority, just the beginning of a long journey to spiritual maturity, and not the end all and be all of lore. No matter the bells and whistles that accompany an opening to higher frequencies, the individual must engage in a lengthy process of integrating the emotional, psychological and spiritual aspects of their being with a higher vibrational level. This process continues throughout their lifetime. No one is ever 'done,' so don't let others fool you into thinking they are godlike, only here to serve your enlightenment, or have achieved a final state. It is beliefs such as these that allow intelligent adults to sacrifice their freedom and independent judgment to people whom they imagine are enlightened.

Once you understand that you cannot recognize a human vibration higher than your own, you see that your concept of enlightenment is the result of cultural and spiritual programming. Real enlightenment may not resemble any of your ideas of it, nor be obvious to you in the least when present in another person. The most revered Indian gurus, with their long white beards, robes, ashrams and large number of disciples, are in costume, fulfilling an age-old need to be a mirror for those craving unconditional love from another human being in the guise of their seeking enlightenment through a guru. The follower's intense adoration of the guru, which grew in their imagination through beliefs in the other's perfection and devotion, and which is magnified by the group mentality, produces its own high. The additional hopeful belief that association with this wise master will increase their own spiritual growth and make enlightenment more likely, is a further source of the disciple's high. But ideas and imagination are not reality, and this seeming spiritual high is sourced in and dependent solely on the continuing relationship with the guru. True spiritual growth is always an internal matter between you and your higher self.

What we may glean from this is that the awakened kundalini may happen to any and all degrees, varying with each new experience of it, and that it has no ability to make a bad person good or a stupid person smart. What it can do, however, is increase your vibration such that more truth becomes available to you. In its highest form, this truth may inform all that you do, casting a new light on your motives, actions and existing abilities, and in some cases elevating your talents to a higher octave of expression. This enhancement may or may not be noted by others, and rarely assures success or recognition in the human scene. Though transformed and awake, you still must 'chop wood and carry water.'

Is kundalini the devil? Or is the devil the many false beliefs about kundalini and the denial of what it really is? Higher awareness reveals that we exist within an ocean of infinite spiritual energy, which we draw from at the level of our own consciousness. Some religious leaders fear the loss of control over their congregation if members could independently access higher frequencies and discover the true nature of reality. This encourages obfuscating and demonizing higher knowledge, and projecting all manner of evil mythologies onto the most natural process of Life. By denying the energy that constitutes our very being, and within which we live, move and have our being, we deny our own Life Force. The awakening of kundalini is simply the awakening to greater frequencies of our own Life Force.

The only danger posed by kundalini is our fear of it, our fear of the unknown which must be confronted whenever we journey into higher planes of consciousness or romance the higher spiritual energies. When we understand that kundalini is our birthright, that we are already and forever immersed in it like a fish in the ocean, and that our interest in it represents a readiness to play with some aspect of these energies, we go into the practice that follows in later chapters with greater confidence. We recognize that we are protected by our own consciousness, that our own readiness level will determine the experience we have, and that we are able to stop the experience at any time if we feel uncomfortable. Whatever unfolds for you is the degree of awakening, or lack of same, prepared by your own higher self. Wisdom means accepting the experience as is – most commonly a pleasurable adventure into the higher energies within your own being, yielding memorable light, thoughts, sensations and imagery.

For the best experience, raising kundalini energy requires a sound mind and body. Please note that we do not recommend this practice if you are suffering from or have suffered from mental illness and/or are on any psychotropic medication. We also do not recommend attempting to raise kundalini while taking mind-altering drugs or while addicted to drugs or alcohol and still using. We further do not recommend this practice for those who are physically ill and/or taking medication for a physical illness, or have weak or debilitated physical bodies. Please make sure to read Chapter Eight, "Is This Technique For You?" for more information before embarking on this journey.

Chapter 4

Understanding the Chakras

There are seven primary chakras or energy centers in the human body. Because you will be flowing sexual energy through your chakras while practicing the 7 Sacred Steps technique taught in the following chapters, it is important to understand how they operate.

Each chakra is associated with a different part of the body and reflects a state of balance or imbalance. An imbalance in any of the chakras may affect certain emotional and physical functions, depending on the part of the body that is involved. Just as each chakra is distinct, the methods that help unblock the chakras are distinct from each other. While you may already be practicing one or more techniques that are useful for restoring balance (such as yoga), by applying the methods discussed below you can tailor your practice even further to achieve specific results.

The First Chakra, otherwise known as the Root Chakra, is located at the base of the spine. It is associated with identity, physical survival and grounding in the earth. It is identified with the earth element and the color red. This chakra focuses on basic survival needs – food, shelter, and safety. It is associated with the parts of the physical body from the base of the spine (coccyx) down through the legs and feet, and also in-cludes the large intestine. When balanced, this chakra allows an individual to feel grounded, safe and secure. An imbalance in this chakra may occur when an individual becomes destabilized due to a change affecting their usual sense of security. For example, a life crisis such as a job loss or loss of a home can shake a person's sense of security and cause an imbalance. Physical manifestations of imbalance include bladder problems, constipation, fatigue, or anemia. Imbalance may also be manifested in behaviors like greed or hoarding as those behaviors are linked to feelings of insecurity. Engaging in yoga, meditation or a walk in nature can unblock this chakra and connect you with the earth.

The Second Chakra, otherwise known as the Navel Chakra, is located right below the navel. It is the center of sexuality, sensuality and creativity. This chakra is associated with the color orange and with the element of water. And just like water flows, this chakra allows for emotional and sensual movement in our lives. The body parts linked to this chakra include the hips, sacrum, lower back, genitals, womb, bladder, and kidneys. When this chakra is in balance, an individual tends to be honest and authentic about their desires and need for intimacy. This chakra is easily pushed out of balance in our modern culture as individuals may come from a background where their sexuality was repressed or where there was too much focus on sexuality. Physical manifestations of imbalance may include feeling numb and out of touch with yourself or having a sex or substance addiction. Certain yoga poses and relaxing near open water can help heal this chakra.

The Third Chakra, also known as the Solar Plexus Chakra, is located above the navel, directly below the breastbone. It is the center of personal power. This chakra is associated with the color yellow and the fire element. It manages self-esteem and warrior energy. Since this chakra is linked to the parts of the body around the solar plexus, including the stomach, small intestines and liver, it also affects bodily functions like digestion and metabolism. When this chakra is balanced, an individual has an appropriate ability to take risks, be assertive, assume responsibility for their own actions, and overcome inertia. The chakra is out of balance when an individual takes too many risks or allows others to violate his or her boundaries. Digestive problems or eating disorders are physical manifestations of imbalance. Spending time in the sun and practicing yoga can restore balance.

The Fourth or Heart Chakra is located in the middle of the chest. It is the center of love and compassion. It links the lower three chakras associated with the world of matter with the upper three chakras that are associated with the world of spirit. This chakra encompasses the heart, upper chest and upper back. The Heart Chakra is tied to the element of air and the color green. A balanced Fourth Chakra allows an individual to connect with peace and harmony, giving love and compassion to others. A deficiency in this chakra can manifest as shyness and loneliness, or a lack of empathy or forgiveness. The physical manifestation of imbalance can appear as shortness of breath or other breathing difficulties. Practicing gratitude, forgiveness, and heart-opening yoga poses can restore balance.

The Fifth or Throat Chakra is located in the middle of the throat. It is the center of self-expression and communication. The Fifth Chakra is the first of the three higher spiritual centers, which include the sixth and seventh chakras. Associated with the color turquoise or blue and the element of sound, this chakra encompasses the neck, throat, jaw and mouth. The sounds that we produce create vibrations that affect our body and the external world. When properly balanced, this chakra allows an individual to clearly communicate with others and express their feelings as needed. An imbalance in this chakra can lead to either too little talking in the case of a deficiency or, in the case of excess, too much talking. A physical manifestation of imbalance can involve an overactive or underactive thyroid. Aromatherapy, speaking to others in a heartfelt way, or journaling are among the practices that may help restore balance to this chakra.

The Sixth or Third Eye Chakra is located between and slightly above the eyebrows. It is the center of inner vision and intuitive perception. It is associated with clairvoyance, telepathy, intuition, dreaming, imagination, and visualization. Traditionally, it includes the ability to visualize positive mental images or symbols while in a deep level of meditation in order to purify harmful karma. The Sixth Chakra is represented by the color indigo and the element of light, and is associated with the pituitary and pineal glands. A balanced Sixth Chakra gives clear thought and vision. Too much energy in this chakra brings headaches, nightmares, and lack of concentration. With a deficient chakra, individuals suffer from memory problems, eye problems and difficulties creating positive visualizations that help focus the mind on purifying images. Visualizing positive images or practicing other visualization techniques can restore this chakra.

The Seventh or Crown Chakra is located at the top and center of the head, and connects with Cosmic Consciousness. This chakra is associated with the color white, which is actually not a color but a reflection of all visible wavelengths of light. The color deep purple has been attributed to this chakra as well. Correlated with the element of thought, the Seventh Chakra deals with the brain and nervous system, and governs the higher mental functions. A balanced chakra is manifested by a strong empathy for others and connection with your spirituality. With too much of this chakra, a person may come across as being judgmental or as having a superiority complex. With a deficiency, a person may appear apathetic and lacking in spirituality. Meditation is often used to bring this chakra into balance.

Take a moment to review the chakras and locate these areas on your own body. Begin with the first chakra and end with the seventh. As you go through each chakra, consider whether any of the previously described signs of imbalance are manifesting in your body or behavior. You can decide to take a small step such as a walk or a few minutes of meditation in order to bring more balance and wellness to your life. Realigning your centers of energy will have a concrete positive impact on your day-to-day functioning as well as improve your overall spiritual well-being.

In the next chapter, we begin our preparations for the Seven Step journey.

Chapter 5

Creating the Right Atmosphere

I'm sure you are already familiar with the importance of setting the mood before having sex with your partner. For this exercise, you will set the stage whether or not you are with a partner. Sacred sex is just as or even more powerful if practiced alone. And I strongly recommend that the first time you try this technique, you do it alone.

Make arrangements to be undisturbed for several hours or more. You need to relax in a private, quiet environment that enhances your senses and encourages a feeling of well-being. The more you relax, the more easily you will move into a state of consciousness that supports your sacred sexual experience.

Gather together the following:

* Candles or other romantic lighting

* Your favorite soft music

* A favorite aroma such as the scent of roses or of jasmine incense (optional)

* Massage oil

* Towels to wipe your hands

* Adjust room temperature to allow you to feel comfortable without clothing

* A comfortable bed with sufficient pillows.

After the candles are lit, the music is playing, the incense or other aroma is released, the temperature has been set, the massage oil and towels laid out and the bed made comfortable, you are ready to begin.

Chapter 6

The Seven Sacred Steps

These are the basic instructions for a solo practitioner. If you are doing this with a partner, return to this chapter after reading "Taking the Seven Steps with a Partner."

Remove all of your clothes. At this point, make any further adjustments to room temperature to ensure your warmth and comfort.

Sit or lie down on the bed and gently massage your legs or any tense areas of your body with warm massage oil for ten minutes or until you feel sufficiently relaxed.

Step One: Stimulation of the Root Chakra
Lie down on your back and, using one or both hands, begin to slowly and rhythmically stimulate your genitals.

Enjoy the feeling as the pleasure builds, but it is essential that you do not allow yourself to orgasm. The intense sexual energy in your genital area is the fuel that will drive the mind-blowing bliss and ecstasy of the kundalini orgasm yet to come. If you feel close to orgasming at any point, slow down.

Step Two: Stimulation of the Navel Chakra
Allow one hand to continue stimulating your genitals while the other hand gently massages your lower abdomen, as if to move the sexual energy up from your genitals to your navel. As the energy reaches and fills your abdomen, continue to massage the area over your navel, taking time to savor the unique sensations. But be very careful not to allow your genital stimulation to trigger an orgasm.

The goal is to flow your sexual energy into each of your chakras as you drive the energy upward toward the highest center of your body for release.

Step Three: Stimulation of the Solar Plexus Chakra

You will now begin moving energy from your navel area to the solar plexus by massaging and gently pushing the energy upwards through the center of your upper abdomen to the breastbone where the solar plexus lies.

You may continue to stimulate your genitals with one hand while using the other to move the energy upwards into your solar plexus. Or you may try stimulating the navel area with one hand while you move the energy into your solar plexus with the other. You can always return to stimulating the genital region at any time if a stronger sexual charge is needed.

Step Four: Stimulation of the Heart Chakra

When the energy has spread fully into the solar

plexus region, you can then continue massaging the area and moving the energy up to the heart chakra in the same way. It is not necessary to maintain stimulation of the genitals if energy is flowing strongly into the higher centers. In this case, one hand stimulates the heart chakra while the other hand massages the solar plexus or navel chakras.

Stimulation of the Heart Chakra may elicit strong emotion, possibly accompanied by rapid breathing and tears, culminating in a deep emotional release. Don't be afraid of these feelings, just allow them to express. Your kundalini orgasm is reaching spiritual ignition at this point.

Step Five: Stimulation of the Throat Chakra
Continue gentle massage of your chest and throat as you move the energy up into the center of your throat. The Fifth or Throat Chakra should be lightly touched, as should the next two higher chakras, which require far less stimulation than the lower ones. At this level, genital stimulation is no longer needed and you may use both hands

to gently activate this center. But be reminded that you can always return to stimulating the genitals whenever you need to, to intensify your energy high.

Step Six: Stimulation of the Third Eye Chakra
When you reach the Third Eye Chakra, you may prefer to sense or inwardly feel into the energy rather than touch the area as it is an extremely sensitive chakra that requires little physical stimulation. Be prepared for exalted visions and transcendent spiritual experiences that will astound and delight you. You are soaring beyond space and time and should allow yourself to remain in this blissful state for as long as desired.

Step Seven: Stimulation of the Crown Chakra
When you are ready to continue, gently direct the energy into your Crown Chakra, at the center and top of your head, for the crowning glory – a rapturous experience so sublime, you will never be the same. Let your whole body dissolve into

blinding Light as you become one with the Universe in ecstatic spiritual surrender.

Chapter 7

Taking the 7 Steps with Your Partner

The Seven Sacred Steps to Kundalini Orgasm technique can be used with your partner. In this instance, your partner relaxes on his or her back and allows you to apply the steps as described in the previous chapter, "The Seven Sacred Steps." This means that you will provide slow and rhythmic stimulation to their chakras as you bring them through the entire experience.

But be advised, working with a partner requires extreme sensitivity and open communication at every stage. Sacred sex and the kundalini orgasm is a timeless experience, therefore, it must never be rushed. Nor must communication ever be forced.

Know in advance that when a person reaches the higher levels of bliss, the experience takes over and communication becomes less and less possible. So let your intuition guide you. In this, as in most things, practice makes perfect!

For the facilitator (giver) of a kundalini orgasm, a truly sublime experience awaits you in witnessing your partner's ecstasy. Invariably, this process results in greater closeness and oneness of the couple when properly carried out by two caring people. No one returns from this transformational journey unchanged, and neither will you nor your partner.

Chapter 8

Is This Technique For You?

Many people feel uncomfortable, or even frightened, when considering a new sexual technique, much less a technique that also involves spiritual expansion. Fear of the unknown has always been a powerful barrier to growth in a human being, and it is no less prevalent when contemplating the total spiritual surrender of a kundalini orgasm with its new sensations and imagery.

Going into it, you don't really know what it will feel like, what will happen to you and whether you will be okay. If you're sharing this technique with a partner, you may wonder whether you're doing it right, whether you will know what to do as the experience progresses and whether your partner will ultimately enjoy the experience.

Your fears and concerns are completely normal and understandable. You would not be human if you did not question whether this technique is for you and/or your partner and whether both of you are in the right frame of mind to take this on at this time.

Our hearts and bodies are not always ready for the adventures our minds are eager to undertake. So before attempting the seven steps, you would be wise to objectively assess where you're at right now. If you are eager to experience this technique but notice that you or your partner can't seem to get to it, there's always something coming up, something in the way, it probably signifies subconscious resistance.

Resistance arises as a response to fear. While it's sometimes wise to push through fear in order to get to the next level, fear can also be an accurate barometer of where you're at, a kind of stop sign telling you that it's not the right time to be exploring your consciousness at this depth.

Consider that maybe this isn't the right time to push the envelope in your sexual/spiritual expression. You can always take up the 7 steps when your inner inspiration and motivation tell you, nay compel you, to give it a shot. That inner voice cannot be denied as it is the compass of your true self.

Some states of mind, such as following a great loss or prolonged emotional stress, can leave you in a fragile state requiring time and healing. If you are seeing a therapist and/or taking psychotropic medication, which may include anti-depressants, anti-psychotics, or tranquilizers, get approval from your therapist or doctor before attempting the 7 step process. Similarly, if your physical health is in any way compromised, consult with your doctor before doing this work. Finally, as mentioned in an earlier chapter, this undertaking requires a sound mind and body, and should not occur while under the influence of mind-altering substances.

If you're feeling vulnerable or unwell and have not been given your doctor's approval, or are not quite ready to unwrap the supreme gift to yourself that is the kundalini orgasm, then continue to wait for as long as you need to. In other words, don't force yourself, put yourself down, or make this another 'to do' in the headlong dash to the finish line of life. Everything happens in its own right time. Know that it will always be there for you if and when you are truly ready.

On the other hand, some of you may need just a little nudge to get past your fear. If so, then consider that the experience of sacred sex and the expansion into the spiritual realms is always cradled in love and light. You will not experience more than you are able to process in that session. You will be able to stop the experience at any time, although I strongly doubt you will want to.

By going with the flow of your own sexual energy as it rises through the chakras and out through the top of your head, you will be amazed at the ecstasy that awaits and delighted by this glimpse into eternity. At the very least, your faith in life will be renewed. Your respect for your body as containing a pathway to the universe will be enhanced. Finally, many 7-steppers also undergo a lasting transformation at the core of their identity, an awakening to their true self that is the stuff of enlightenment.

Whatever your experience is, have no doubt that in undertaking this magical journey you will come face to face with "O Magnum Mysterium," the great mystery, and you will not return un-changed.

Parting Thoughts

Because I don't personally know you, kind reader, much less how you are interpreting or applying this information, I can make no guarantees that you or your partner will reach the transcendent spiritual/sexual bliss of a kundalini orgasm.

However, I can promise that a sacred journey of ecstatic exploration lies ahead of you, and I recommend that you approach this as you would a sacred journey – with courage and respect.

It all begins with a single step. After that, you need only take another small step, and then yet another, until before you know it, you are delivered to the most exquisite joy and bliss that is available to a human being in this life.

Before you go, please make sure to contact us for your free gift, the two-book starter library, "Practical Lessons in Yoga" and "Meditation Made Easy." These ebooks are the perfect complement to *Sex Yoga*. They will teach you how to quiet your mind, focus in the moment, strengthen your core and consciously move energy through your chakras. This will help assure your success with the technique you have learned in *Sex Yoga* and prepare you for the powerful energetic changes that occur when you attempt to raise your kundalini.

To receive your free gift, just send an email to info@diamondstarpress.com with your proof of purchase and "Send Sex Yoga Gift" in the subject field, and we will get your bonus ebooks out to you right away. Do it now before you forget!

Did You Enjoy This Book?

Dear Reader,

Thank you for reading *Sex Yoga: The 7 Easy Steps to a Mind-Blowing Kundalini Awakening!* I hope you enjoyed it. My purpose in writing this book is to introduce you to the mind-expanding power of sacred sex so that you, or you and your partner, may find sexual/spiritual healing and awakening through the seven step technique.

If you would like to recommend this book to other readers, please write a review on Amazon. It will only take a few minutes, and I would appreciate it immensely.

Thanks again, and wishing you the very best!

S. F. Howe

Books by S. F. Howe

MIND · BODY · SPIRIT

HIGHER CONSCIOUSNESS

Matrix Man: How To Become Enlightened, Happy And Free In An Illusion World

The author reveals a new reality paradigm that will liberate you from the limiting beliefs and programs that prevent a joyful and fulfilling life. Available in print and digital editions.

The Top Ten Myths Of Enlightenment: Exposing The Truth About Spiritual Enlightenment That Will Set You Free!

Essential reading for spiritual seekers. What no one else will tell you to help you avoid the pitfalls of the spiritual journey. Available in print and digital editions.

The Bringer: How To Free Yourself From The Mind Control Programs Of The Matrix Reality

Available in print and digital editions.
Coming Soon!

PLANT INTELLIGENCE

Secrets Of The Plant Whisperer: How To Care For, Connect, And Communicate With Your House Plants

A plant whisperer reveals the hidden truth about plants and why relating to them in a conscious way is vital for their health and well-being. Available in print and digital editions.

Your Plant Speaks!: How To Use Your Houseplant As A Therapist

Let your house plant solve your problems! Discover the little known art of receiving life coaching from your favorite indoor plant.
Coming Soon!

PERSONAL GROWTH

Vision Board Success: How To Get Everything You Want With Vision Boards!

A powerful technique for achieving your goals and manifesting your desires. Available in print and digital editions.

Sex Yoga: The 7 Easy Steps To A Mind-Blowing Kundalini Awakening!

A technique for activating the chakras to induce a powerful kundalini experience. Available in print and digital editions.

Morning Routine For Night Owls: How To Supercharge Your Day With A Gentle Yet Powerful Morning Routine!

Morning rituals aren't only for morning people, and they don't have to be rough and tumble or performed at top speed to set up a perfect day. Welcome to the world of the gentle yet powerful wake-up routine for night owls! Available in print and digital editions.

CONSCIOUS HEALTH

Transgender America: Spirit, Identity, And The Emergence Of The Third Gender

A higher consciousness perspective on the Transgender Agenda; what it is and why it is being rolled out at breakneck speed to socially engineer a gender dysphoria epidemic. Available in print and digital editions.

When Nothing Else Works: How To Cure Your Lower Back Pain Fast!

The simple method that no doctor will ever tell you about. Requires no drugs, no surgery, and no special equipment. Available in print and digital editions.

About the Author

S. F. Howe is a transformational psychologist, author, screenwriter, musician and spiritual teacher. Howe received a master's degree and doctoral training in clinical psychology, and worked in hospitals and clinics for more than 25 years as a psychotherapist, staff psychologist, clinical program consultant and director of chemical dependency and psychiatric programs.

In the midst of graduate studies, a profound spiritual awakening led to a complete reevaluation of the author's life path. Thus began a spiritual journey along the road less traveled, extending far beyond clinical psychology, conventional reality paradigms and both traditional religion and new age spirituality.

While engaged in a unique, ongoing process of discovery, the author enjoys sharing with others an ever-expanding understanding of the true nature of personal reality. This has resulted in Howe's noted books and teachings on the subjects of higher consciousness, conscious health, personal growth and plant intelligence.

Howe's primary intention is to bring an end to suffering by guiding others on a well-worn path to truth and expanded awareness. Many of those who have experienced Howe's input and presence report emotional and physical healing, life-changing realizations and dramatic personal transformation.

S. F. Howe may be contacted for speaking and teaching engagements. Please direct all inquiries to info@diamondstarpress.com.